Changing carriages at Birmingham New Street

By Andy N:

Return to Kemptown (2010 / Revised 2020)
The End of Summer (2015)
The Birth of Birth (2018)
The Streets were all we could see (2020)
Haiku of Life (2021)
Dock Leaves (2022)
In the Midst of Winter (2022)
From the Diabetic Ward Volume 1 (2023)
Changing carriages at Birmingham New Street (2023)

Split books:

A Means to an End (with Jeff Dawson (2011)
Europa (with Nick Armbrister) (2014)
Europa II (with Nick Armbrister) (2016)
Europa III (with Nick Armbrister) (2018)
Run away with me in 7 words (with Amanda Steel) (2019)
Europa IV (with Nick Armrbister) (2020)
The lockdown was all we could see (with Amanda Steel) (2020)
The winter was all we could see (with Amanda Steel (2021)
Europa V (with Nick Armbrister) (2022)
Europa VI (with Nick Armbrister (2022)
Run away with me again in 8 words (with Amanda Steel) (2022)
Europa VII (with Nick Armbrister) (2023)

The Barbarians of the Wall:

Enemy of the Wall (2018)
Buried alive on the Wall (2020)

Role Reversal:

Night of the Wolf (2017)

Selected Poems:

Selected Poems Volume 1 (2022)
Selected Poems Volume 2 (2023) ** Forthcoming **

Chapbooks:

'Mystery Story (2014)
(http://www.origamipoems.com/poets/211-andy-n)
Selected scenes from the end of the world (2020)
Games People Play (2020)

From Friendship to Love:

From Friendship to love I (2017)
From Friendship to love II (2019)

Non Fiction:

Adventures in sound and music - articles for the Sunday Tribune Volume 1 - 2019 to 2021 (2021)

Changing carriages
at Birmingham New Street

Andy N

All Poems and introductions @ Andy N (aka Andy Nicholson) 2023.

A number of versions these poems have appeared in various books / magazines and Andy N would like to thank the journals / books for publication of these pieces.

All rights are reserved.

No reproduction, copy or transmission of this publication may be made without written permission.

The author has asserted his right to be identified as the authors of this work in accordance with the Copyright, Designs and Patents act 1988.

Published and printed by N Press, Denton, Manchester.

This book was wrote between 2016 to 2023.

Contents

Introduction:

Changing carriages at Birmingham New Street

Moving down South

Infinity and back

Twenty Yards behind

Five yards in front

Five yards behind

Turning back from Fleetwood

Playing Trumpton Cover versions
with Freddie Phillips at the edge of Stonehenge

Unplanned weekend in Blackpool

Hiding in the Black Horse in Farnworth

Homage to Bagpuss in Hove

Homemade Chains and Preston Market

Asleep on Flookburgh Beach with Nick Drake

Remembering your father in Leeds

Your father's records

Piano burial at Morecombe

Accidental drowning at Harold Park

Unexpected change of weather near Jackson's Boat

Over the other side of Winterhill

Above the edge of everything in Hebden Bridge

The Way Through to Bluebell Woods (with apologies to Kipling)

Waiting for the last bus at Seaford

Rainstorm near Todmodern Rail Station

Return to Shipley Woods

Last Junction to Denton

The Night of Whit Parade in Mossley

The day after the Whit Parade in Mossley

Point of No Return

Telling the truth

First Meeting

Homesick

Between yesterday and today, or somewhere further afield

Between then and there, everything disintegrated.

Church Closure at Guide Bridge

Your brother's funeral

Facing Shipley Woods

Your Records

Three visits to Paris ten years apart

After Leaving

Going to your funeral in Radcliffe

Biography

Introduction

The journey from 'Return to Kemptown my first poetry book' to 'Changing Carriages at Birmingham New Street' has been marked by a profound shift, both in my writing style and the themes that stir my creative soul. While 'Dock Leaves,' 'In the Midst of Winter,' and 'From the Diabetic Ward Volume 1' all share in the meticulous crafting process alongside 'The End of Summer' and 'The Birth of Autumn,' it's the complexity of 'Changing Carriages' that stands as a testament to this evolving journey.

As I conclude my journey into the realm off poetry books at least for the moment possibly for good, 'Changing Carriages at Birmingham New Street' stands not only as a culmination of artistic growth but also as a departure from the familiar. While the earlier books were woven from the fabric of my memories and emotions, this final work delves into a narrative tapestry that explores the intricate lives of characters, echoing with the influences of Paul Auster.

The internal conversations within the book, the reflective letters that echo through its pages, and the persistent question "Do you remember, Sarah" serve as not just artistic devices, but as the heartbeat of the work. They give the book its own distinct voice, a voice that accompanies readers on a journey laden with mystery, emotion, and human connection.

Something that will follow no matter what I write next.

Andy N

August 2023

Changing carriages at Birmingham New Street

During those early days, of course
we had to keep it quiet
whether I was stopping at the Malmaison in Leeds,
and you lied about a new client in Horsforth
which went on nearly all night.

And how about that time at Birmingham New Street
when the train broke down
halfway back from Euston
and we ended up sitting in separate carriages
when your husband had to come to get you.

Do you remember Warwick Castle, Sarah
and Manchester United before that Champions
League match
where we could only chat for five minutes
at the beer counter during halftime
to prevent anybody from becoming suspicious,

and the return leg two weeks later in Madrid
which I had to cancel at the last minute
when one of my girls went down ill
just before I was due to leave
and I ended up spending the night in the hospital

Courting our guilt in ways we didn't recognise
from an almost nervous beginning
when we were reconnecting as friends
unlocking our hearts like suitcases
lock after lock after lock

sitting on steps outside Manchester Piccadilly Station
every time we met, sweeping everything else aside
under an imaginary table
openmouthed in sorries
each time we kissed to start with.

Moving down South

Was it when we were 12 or 13, Sarah
when your parents
decided to move house
and only told you the night before
to go and pack your bags.

'It's not far' You told me in my room
'We'll keep in touch.'
even though neither of us
really believed what
the other one of us said.

Who stopped writing first,
I don't remember, do you, Sarah
as I threw myself into my writing
barely into my teens
and you married young.

Too young when your letter
arrived out of the blue
buried under bills
with two girls in tow
and a publisher on my back.

Too young in almost a rhetorical question
carrying your guilt on a platter
and everything that went before
almost like you were
thought I was listening as you wrote,

leaving me stunned to this day
all those years later
when you stumbled back
into my life.

Infinity and back

Do you remember how far back we went, Sarah
before you came back into my life
like stepping back under the hedge
from a different time zone.

Twenty years before, it must have been
you moved away with your parents
only writing to me three weeks after
your words garbled in leaf mould,

Our friendship outweighs our regrets
over occasional letters over the years
when we both got married
and I became a father twice.

I used to imagine you in plays of your own making
tapping your wine cup on the crusp of a stage
never releasing your own real drama
was your only unhappiness,

Moving your toes like seaweed
when in reality you wanted to move like oceans
with a backpass to a completely
different way of looking at things

not a burial ground of your own making
in a code red situation
limping back to where you came from
dragging us both off into infinity.

Twenty Yards behind

Reeling emotions in an afterthought
your second letter followed
before I had a chance to respond
apologising for being so thoughtless
saying you understood
if you didn't want to write back
or if it was simply too busy,

the truth was, Sarah
do you remember me saying
we had been away in a village
its name, which I have since forgotten
twenty yards behind both of my girls
on hired bicycles, helping them prepare
for some big inter-school race,

Unable to walk for two days after
my fingers were red bleeched in sores
in a vain attempt to support my girls
in an upcoming bicycle race
for ten miles each way in a rainstorm
leaving both almost paralysed in laughter
as I struggled to get back into the car,

coddling my emotions in puzzlement
when Melissa said to me afterwards
on the way back home afterwards
only for me to push it back into my pocket
feeling like a child bearing an eraser.
And my interest had been pulled ashore
for the first time in years and years.

Five yards in front

Do you remember me telling you, Sarah
before we met up for the first time in years
I was happily married in my first letter
only realising afterwards
that this was far from the case.

Do you remember that guard? Sarah
at that station, which I walked you onto
when his smile magnestied
as we walked into his booking office
and before the newsagent next door.

Perhaps in hindsight, they knew
more than a few things that either of us knew
or perhaps I was concerned
about my book deal, which was still dangling
half soaked over a cliff,

Perhaps in hindsight they knew
watching you get onto the train
and I walked back onto the lanes
raising my arms up unsure
whether I knew what I was doing,

which I found out afterwards
that I didn't.

Five yards behind

Five yards behind,
half-broken by the wind,
do you remember that seat
outside Bourenmouth Pier
the night after the storm, Sarah
on our second meeting,

Do you remember me saying
it looked like a bird
a few people took it in turns
slowly pulling IT apart
streaking the footpath
into a warning of don't enter.

I remember telling you
the night before, upon parking
I could see the waves writing
a love letter to each other
rising through the fog
through square reflections,

Churning softly in the breeze
cloud-lit in a gap of memory
binding us together
almost straight away
before we even knew it
scattering our emotions in the sand.

Turning back from Fleetwood

It was never easy for me either. Sarah
when we started seeing each other again
from when you used to lie to your husband
before you left him about working late to see me
and I had to say I had been transferred
to another section to get out of
picking up my girls every day from school.

Do you remember, Sarah?
At that time, we were going to meet at
the edge of Manchester Fort
for a long lunch, and I had to avoid it
on next to no notice
when Melissa broke her wrist playing Hockey
and I had to drop everything.

I know it upset you looking back
when I got the phone call, almost literally
as I stepped out of the car to meet you
and I had to go within moments
even after we eventually moved in together
heavy with emotional regret
that still hangs tight in my heart even now.

Do you remember Bradford?
when I had agreed to take them to the film
and photography museum
and we agreed to meet in the bar
in the hotel inn after they fell asleep
only for my wife to ring us up
just after I got there,

and Fleetwood when we had to turn back
years and years later, just halfway to Southport
when Melissa went into labour,
a month and a half earlier than what was expected
with what became her first child
I should have seen it then
laid out as a major warning.

I should have seen what was coming
that evening when you stormed out of my car
leaving me with the choice of them and you
and to this day I don't know how
I persuaded you to get back in there
and come back all the way to
Bolton General Hospital with me.

Seeing that moment as like a reference point
in a map of where not to go in a relationship
looking through a glass darkly
swiping at the leaves in our garden for days after
like a shot from a gun you were let to shoot
turning the corner next with everything we did
like threadbare wishes until it was all gone.

Playing Trumpton Cover versions with Freddie Phillips at the edge of Stonehenge

Wandering through the countryside
whose idea was it to stop a
few miles outside Stonehenge
and sit there that afternoon,
Picnic and acoustic guitars in hand, Sarah
and recreate Freddie Phillips work on Trumpton.

It was never that he lived anywhere near there
but you just wanted to sit near Stonehenge
with my old cassette recorder
lying next to my car
determined to learn a few of his tracks
in a slightly slower key,

F you told me when I stumbled onto E
when we went through the Fireman drill
and I started playing Windy Miller's song afterwards
smiling silently to yourself
after realising I had drunk way too much
for you to get much sense out of me by then.

Mr. Farthing, Mrs. Honeyman, and Mr. Swallow
I tried to keep up with you stumbling
around on my fretboard, imagining I was a genius.
when in reality I was barely an amateur
frost-furred next to our car in a blanket
looking slowly at the sunset.

The past festered in our hearts, counting notes again
in the dawn over the nearby fields
music from our childhood
drawing us both together again,
burying our guitars into our emotions
our love into barelycorn.

Unplanned weekend in Blackpool

Do you remember, Sarah
those purple open windows
in that hotel on Albert Road
and the beer soaked train tickets
tucked into that cup on the table,
when you said you loved me for the first time?

That sunset that lit up the clouds
that made them look on fire
and the rain on the pier
just outside the tower
like bleared music
caught between dusk and dawn.

Madam Tussauds
where you nearly got us thrown out
before pleading with the guard
two hours afterwards
when we missed our train back
to let us sleep on the platform.

Do you remember, Sarah
the receptionist's face at that hotel
when you put the waterworks on
before sneaking me in afterwards
after he took pity on you
and let you stay for nothing.

I can still see the look.
Carried in his eyes
As you smiled
while winking at me to hurry up
like your head was on a stick
half buried in the light.

I refused to say anything
even when you got there ten minutes after me
proclaiming that it was a lucky escape
repeating the Polish, you had just confused him with
all the way into bed
shushing me all night long asleep.

Hiding in the Black Horse in Farnworth

Do you remember the fact
We were still really strangers, Sarah
Not even a couple
When you came to meet me in Farnworth
that lunchtime, just after I returned to work
and we ended up sneaking out of the Black Horse
when my boss walked in
in the middle of my second hour of lunch.

Do you remember telling me in that stark,
knuckle stained light
under my breath
when she walked into the side door
and you saw me go white-faced
"Why don't you tell her the truth?
we had simply lost track of time
rather than just sneak out of the back.

'You must be joking'
my voice crackled under my breath
like a dodgem on a ghost train track
rubbing my nerves
into bite-sharp chunks
and the way you followed me
into the consuming mist
without batting an eyelid.

I can picture you even now
running through the rain
to where we were parked
your hat sank over your nose
carrying your shoes
after they turned into cups of water
and stood there laughing
when we both got back into our cars.

You couldn't have planned it
I remember you saying
who would have thought
she would turn up
when we were in there
laughing to yourself
your laughter carrying across
the rain of emotion,

leaving me unaware
even then
how much impact
you were about to leave
on my life.

Homage to Bagpuss in Hove

Was it the third or fourth night, Sarah?
during that month, we lived in Hove
when my agent paid for us both to
 move there temporary,
that second summer, we were together,
and we stumbled onto that singer
playing alone beside the coastline
at the start of dusk.

Do you remember him asking, Sarah?
pausing in between songs
can either of us play an autoharp
or a mandolin
at the edge of the beach
a cup of hot chocolate
barely keeping
his aged fingers warm.

I'd grown up watching it like you
although I couldn't begin
to name any of the songs
he played one after the other,
rather the names of Bagpuss's friends
from Professor Yaffle to
The Mice on the mouse-organ
to Gabriel the Toad and Madeleine

I see the singer's face even now
haromnica in his mouth
playing a melody of Song of the Flea
and Charliemouse Weaving
before eventually finishing with
the bony king of nowhere
opening up the curtain
to an unexpected love.

You didn't get it, I should have seen
in the ash-coloured light
finding the nostaliga too strange
pausing for a few minutes
as if you were listening to something else
before hurrying on as before
underlining the differences between us both
that I only realised after you had gone.

Homemade Chains and Preston Market

Let's go out the back door.
instead of the front, Sarah
and walk around to our car.
and enjoy the freedom
that summer sunlight
brings us
at the start of June.

Perhaps we can drive down to Lancaster,
and hopefully our car
won't break down again
like it did on the way to Morecombe
and you sat on that bus stop seat
bathing in the sunshine
until the AA man eventually arrived,

or carry on to Preston like last time
Do you remember, Sarah?
and revisit Avenham and Miller Park
buried in tourists
before going back to the market
to see if that old lady was still there
selling those homemade chains.

Do you remember her face
When she said to me
Be careful,
oh god, be careful
when she placed it on your neck
leaving us both wondering for ages
what she was talking about,

postmarking the scene back home
watching our lives from a distance
flashing before us in a restless freedom
our heads floating above water
before the tragedy that came next
shaking everything to a standstill,
when everything went wrong.

Asleep on Flookburgh Beach with Nick Drake

Ricocheting all the back outstretched
from Morecombe Beach
do you remember, Sarah?
Why we went to Flookburgh in error
instead of going back to Manchester?

In hindsight, it was funny when we went past
Oxenholme
and you blurted out, shocked
'We're going completely the wrong way'
and we both just decided to go to Flookburgh
for another night before heading home.

Do you remember that high-built
cloud on the edge of the coastline
all that evening after tea and four glasses of wine
like a postcard from another time
and Nick Drake's three hours ringing in our ears

and the gulls flying off the coastline
into the deep sunset in the distance
leaving us both too tired to look at each other
right up to when the Policeman
woke us both at the crisp of dawn

shifting us along in silence
with the start of the rain
laughing over our mistake
clutched in silence all the way to the car
moored in the jetty early morning fog

and our worries hung like
a strand of cotton
on the edge of a blade
in deep love
right before everything went wrong.

Remembering your father in Leeds

Do you remember that hotel near Fort William, Sarah?
that we visited on our honeymoon
and your brother, who rang me up at midnight
in a panic-stricken call about your father
who had been found dead in bed.
with Mrs. Cooper from Number Seven?

Do you remember reminding me on the way back?
when I met him at your nephew's christening.
and he spent over an hour asking me
about the three poetry books I had released.
and why I wasn't writing more like Tennyson
than, in his words, any of that modern crap.

Truth be told, I didn't really remember that day
even when your brother found out about my love of jazz
asked me to go and look through his rare vinyl
which I found was more Harry Secombe than Miles Davies
and Michael Bolton than John Coltrane
that left me breathing no, no, no, no throughout.

How long had he been seeing Mrs. Cooper
it was hard to judge, your brother told us afterwards.
after we arrived in the middle of the night
but he suspected it had been going on for years.
right up to when he died in the middle of
what he said was frisky business.

He was a remarkable man, as you told everybody at the funeral
but a total bastard to your mother

in the hotel afterwards to me in a food of tears
shocked that both he and Mrs. Cooper had managed
to keep it hidden from both of their families.
as long as the pair of them had managed.

Cursing yourself for weeks afterwards when we got home
that none of the four of you
had spotted something was wrong
and it only came out after he died
conjuring chaos from an emotional moment
but they had effectively been living a lie for years.

Changing everything overnight for all of you
into an uneven, flagged footpath of memories
with rows that went on for years with your sisters
and your brother, who descended into alcoholism
leaving you with emotional codes of regret.
We couldn't decode it until it was too late.

Your father's records

It wasn't much to show, was it, Sarah?
for a lifetime's shopping
just a few classic albums from your dad
the rest being sold off for beers
when your mum stopped his beer tab
which your older sister
dropped off in a box without stopping.

I felt sorry for them
do you remember me telling you, Sarah
covered in fingerprints
clearly dragged off to the local record shop
and placed back on the shelf there
when nobody clearly would touch them
or deal with his abusive behaviour,

making me recall the way he must have felt
when he bought them originally
before he started cheating on your mum
and started spending
more and more money in the pub
and ignoring all of you
as you grew up and needed him,

perched in his emotions
when he put them back in a huff afterwards
almost like Al Green's 'Call me, come back home'
or Simple Mind's 'Don't you (forget about you)
clearly skipping through his thoughts
when he then died in his mistress's arms,

saying that my memories are now yours.

Piano burial at Morecombe

Do you remember that old man and his son
who dragged out that old piano in front of us
to the seafront at Morecombe, Sarah
and then proceed to throw it
piece by piece into the Ocean
after spending an hour chopping it up.

'Shut up and keep cutting it'
Do you remember the older man saying
'We don't have any all day
it's what she would have wanted'
before watching it drift into the ocean
as it merged with decades old wood.

Their heads disappearing
into the hats
as the rain came down halfway
forcing us both back inside my car
leaving us wondering afterwards
did they finish it?

It must have been for his mother
you proclaimed on the way back home
burying her piano in a silent tribune
like a library of stones into the sea
carried away with the tidal cycle
reeled with some kind of personal memory.

I only found out after you had gone
they did it when they found out
she wasn't coming out of the hospital
and would never play for them again
over breakfast or supper
before their son went to bed

funnelling south in her dreams
across Waleny Lighthouse as a childhood
throwing her arms out freely
into a fraying seam of two worlds colliding
burying herself, following others dreams
like you did with us without realising it.

Accidental drowning at Harold Park

Drifting across the water
why did you think it was a body? Sarah
rather than just an odd-shaped
piece of broken wood
floating in the middle of the lake?

Headfirst, it looks like somebody
had jumped into the lake
you proclaimed until you realised otherwise
and pushed their head in
until they could no longer breath.

Enwreathing itself in your childhood fears
when Blondie, your mum's dog
had raced into the lake when you took her out
after school when you were 12
only to nearly see her drown in front of you.

Chasing your stick, you said you stood there
you knew she liked chasing sticks
and watched in horror as she slipped
at the edge of the lake
and didn't come back up.

You never found out the name of the man
who grabbed her out almost by instinct
somehow without slipping
in out-stretched fingers
turning everything around in seconds.

Hitch-hiking through your own memories
at least twenty years
as you fell into my arms
as you proclaimed
how you could never tell anybody.

Centrefold in your own guilt
when you got her home
still half drenched in the water,
barely able to lie
she had been rolling in the snow

wearing your lies in your guilt silently
you had been unable to pull Blondie
out of that lake like a coat
which had more pockets
that you could never tell any of them

snagged between a trigger
of helplessness and fear for years afterwards
left in a corner of your memories
as much a hint of darkness in a yard of light
you were never able to rush into that lake

mirrored when you saw yourself in your father
upon reflection of his affairs
when we first got together
and you were unable to tell any of your family
about us for months and months.

Unexpected change of weather near Jackson's Boat

Left dangling in the wind, the gate behind us
was left dangling open, wasn't it, Sarah?
as a final learning curve
after we passed through it
beckoning us to come back to it
and try to shut it again.

Digging a way through the air to another world
we had just been left behind
quivering on the other side of the river
between now and then
bresting the horizons
with the change in weather.

Lapping on auto-pilot
all the way to the next field
our feet are covered in ice-laced leaves
and legs in ash-coloured shadows
mid-stride running back
in a soft trot to your car.

Dissecting emotions left out for a eulogy
through another field, then another
implanting silent notes of music
over your car window like magic
as the snow signalled the end of Autumn
all the way home.

Over the other side of Winterhill

Rustling in the wind
the closer we got to the other side of the Winterhill, Sarah
your scrawled message of goodbye
played deep on both of our consciences.
the longer you stopped at the barbed wire fence
that led to the cliff towards the sea
watching a gull
then two fly out into the early, hazy morning sun.

Where they had come from
neither of us were sure
whether from a cave
further down the cliff, out of our eyes.
heeded in the loose cloak of mist
or perhaps had been sitting in
on one of the gaps on the edge
like they were on a loose boundary wall.

Dispelling your intended words
as you threw his ashes into the breeze
into a new meaning of sparse anger
towards both of your brother and sisters
who would have nothing to do with him
when everybody had found out
about his affair after he died
leaving you with no choice.

No choice in the early morning light
right up to when the gulls flew straight up
after you scattered his ashes
like a memory crumbling at the edge
and their cries
carrying both you and
wherever he went to next
to a new beginning.

Above the edge of everything in Hebden Bridge

Let us go then, you and me, to Hebden Bridge, Sarah
with your bright blue hair, which stands out like a beacon
across the moonlight in the park opposite the station
and laugh at ourselves in the windows at Greens
where last time we saw your ex with a much younger date
and how he didn't come running out in anger I don't know.

Lose ourselves in rare books from the book case on Market Steet
which I doubt either of us will ever read in twenty years
and then change our minds at least four times in Silly Billys
about what I should buy Melanie and Michelle
before eventually giving up altogether when the owner suggests
they are more likely to be into boys now than dolls.

Attempt to find those hills in Heptonstall
your father promised he would take you
every time you went past there as a child
when he would take you on the way to York
just before Christmas with both of your sisters
and then forget when they started arguing again.

Go to the Picturehouse to see Pain and Glory.
and stop for a coffee at the Organic House Cafe
if we couldn't be bothered with a glass of wine
spinning ourselves out of our shadows of a normal
weekend
like a tiny, winged ghost above the edge of everything
free from everything for just the afternoon.

The Way Through to Bluebell Woods (with apologies to Kipling)

Half baked in your brother's cheap brandy
can you remember who counted the cobblestones first?
at the top of his garden, near his kitchen door
that led to his back gate
then multiplied it by twenty
before you proclaimed it wouldn't come close
to walk through the forest
that eventually led back to the train station.

Do you remember Sarah, who suggested
we go for a walk in that forest beyond that gate
and paused at that broken down log
on the other side of the fence
covered in sideward shadows
that led to the gap in-between the forest
which stood there looking
like a deserted airport.

Discharging nature, everything we saw
into a hazy reflection
like we were standing on a glass roof
listening to birds cheeping over
his neighbour's farm house
and a cock getting confused
with the change in season.

Carrying everything back
into a hazy comparison across the shadows
with your brother's pounding house music
stood there, looking into the distance
making a different meaning of
the way everything looked
whether drunk or sober
and whether it was a hundred steps or ten

hiding your demons about your Dad
for just one night
before everything went horrific.

Waiting for the last bus at Seaford

Beating our teeth in the wind
our relationship began
stringing lies to everybody in a diary-like fashion
so nobody knew what was going on
no matter where we were
or wasn't as the case sometimes turned out to be.

Do you remember that first night, Sarah?
when you texted me on the train to Brighton
saying you weren't really sure about this
only to turn up when I had finished my coffee
and was reaching for my coat
to walk down to the seafront,

and that second night
when we got the bus down to Seaford
and we wandered without direction
trying to find the white chalk cliffs
and you wouldn't hold my hand, saying
'We don't know who we will bump into'.

I didn't love you then
ducking in and out of the fog
speaking softly to reassure you
I knew where we were going
all the way back to the bus stop
when in reality, I was as lost as you.

I didn't have the heart to tell you then
although I had been there before
I certainly wasn't an expert and just smiled
What are we going to do if the bus
doesn't turn up or has failed early'
framing my phone into an amber beacon

exposing both of our shaking in images
instead of fragmented attempts at humour
until our bus eventually turned up
tracing the creases of disillusion
pulling us both together like cars
just before crashing without realising.

Rainstorm near Todmodern Rail Station

Breathing into each other's faces,
Do you remember Sarah
The light irradiating as soon as
As we left the station that morning
Then dissolving into a thunderstorm
And we were both left there
Undecided, what should we should do next.

Do you remember the guard
Looking at us as we stood there
Like, we were just plain daft
as we stood at the edge of the waiting room
watching the rain come down
with a gentle tap, telling us in an ancient language
to forget about going any further.

Perhaps if we had been there separately
We would either just go for it
And we ran to where we were going
No matter how heavy the rain
Or just given up and gone back home
On the next train back to Manchester
In a crushing disappointment

But together, we were left
astounded by the beauty of the water
Gaping wider and wider by the minute
Afraid to break the silence
Until it finished at its own natural pace
Unaware life was about to pull us back to normality
without even realising it.

Return to Shipley Woods

If I could ever meet you again, Sarah
You know, I would suggest walking again
across Shipley Woods to the Tame
until we come near the boundary
just across the road from Guide Bridge Train Station.

Do you remember the boundary that afternoon?
When you walked out in front of the waitress
in their restaurant wing
and stormed up the road up to the Queen's Arms
claiming that place was haunted.

The Queens were packed out; do you remember
and we ended up getting two cheese and onion
butties
from Kevins, just up the road
before you suggested, why don't we
go for a stroll around Shipley Woods.

Do you remember our house
and the first time we came across it
after stumbling out of the woods
and spending ten minutes debating
about going into the Sun.

I wanted to carry on up the road
and go to the Pack Horse knowing it would be quieter
but you were determined to go into the Sun
'I ain't going to any old man's drinking pub'
proclaiming with an steely eyed determination.

Perhaps if I had put my foot down
we would have gone to the Pack Horse
and never come back to Guide Bridge again
apart from seeing your brother
on the other side of Crown Point North

unfolding our relationship without realising
when you saw the sign for sale outside
as if immobilised by forces beyond our control
clawing through my soul even now
reflecting in backward shadows

buried deep within another lifetime
when you looked at me and said
'should we? Could we? Would it be a good idea?
racing emotions across the pathway
leading to the front door,

returning to my thoughts even now, years after
should we? Could we? Would it be a good idea?
cast out across the air like discarded lines from
poems
wasted across my regrets in vulnerable sounds
killing everything without realising when I said yes.

Last Junction to Denton

Where has the snow come from?
do you remember saying to me, Sarah
that last evening, I picked you up from work,
halfway down Hyde Road
wondering had it been waiting for us
to both head home
or something.

re-interpreting your emotions
metamorphosing between the moon
and the rising sun
the nearer as we
drove past the Apollo
then the Old Showcase
and Tescos in Gorton

rolling off the undercurrent
next to the Sainsburys
and the KFC on the Rock
leading past St. George's Church
into the snow near Dominos
on Manchester Road
when it came down out of nowhere.

Where has that come from?
do you remember saying
as we got home
at the edge of Shepley Woods
watching it pull itself up
towards the tame
before suddenly cutting off.

I don't know
I tried smiling back
rolling back time even now
bucking the light
as I slowly pulled up
lost in your slight sigh
leaving clues like a note in a bottle,

unaware until you walked out
two hours later
leaving your footprints
all the way up to the forest
almost like you were
following your father beyond his death
unable to tell me,

veiled to your past.

The Night of Whit Parade in Mossley

Half baked in four or
was it five pints of Builders Crac
and True Grit we had
the night before things went mad
and we collapsed outside
Mossley Parnish,

do you remember Sarah?
me dancing all over the small walls
to the brass bands throughout the day
while you sat there,
head in your hands
barely able to hold back your anger

simmering in an alocholic slush
and tar starred ale
which started all the way down
from the Rising Sun to the Dog and Partridge
and wherever we went after
that should have been just one pint.

glittering circular
to the ale and the music
from sunset to almost sunrise
kissing away in the ambience
like Angels tied in chains
the more and more wild it got

brushing each other awake
in the early morning breeze
elbowing hangovers
bruised words into spells
barely able to stand up
until we had two coffees each

and I collapsed an hour later
on the Moors
changing everything forever.

The day after the Whit Parade in Mossley

Heading up into the moors
the day after the Whit Parade
half-cooked from too much alcohol
do you remember telling me? Sarrah
never, ever again

stripped of emotion
bent double in the sun
vacant among sombre fields
hand in hand with dried lilacs
your face white as a sheet,

over the apple trees
on the other side
of the closed-off form
jinked in the undergrowth of mud
where I collapsed

fanning the ambience
with your legs screaming constantly
stretched out across thistles and nettles
over the top of rust-locked gates
where you tried to get me to sit down,

sulking all the way over the hills
and wet almost right through
on the way back
when it started raining
thinking I was just hungover,

romancing the air
with an air of constant earache
until you got me home
and it became apparent
I was now diabetic.

Point of No Return

Looking back at photographs
we were never at home in our first flat
were we Sarah?

Magnetising moments in reflection
from your red raincoat fracturing the door
when the door peg collapsed.

Rising your smile close to tears
stood next to that fridge
which never worked properly.

In my dreams,, there is still a rope
between the pair of us like the wind
constantly pulling at the windows.

Something that was anchored there
bearing an eraser at the point of no return
when we left our partners,

tearing us apart slowly
without us realising it
as we moved in together.

Telling the truth

Do you remember how long it was, Sarah?
before I could tell both of my girls about us?
Was it six or twelve months after both
of our marriages had finally failed,
and you brought us together like a beacon spell?

Mine was harder, of course.
considering We had been together for 14 years
and I had both of the girls to think about
but you just walked out unexpectedly.
you told me that night.

He had had it coming for years,
do you remember texting me
had been a prick to you for years
concluding, "I couldn't take it,
I couldn't take it anymore."

Mine was more complex; it always was
but the girl's mom, my then-wife, always knew
completing my sentence before I finished it
'You've met somebody else, haven't you?'
telling the truth before I could ever say,

Mine was more complex, it always was
almost like a memory of keys afterwards
tied up before and after we met
leaving me afraid to face my fears
holding my head afterwards with tears,

unaware of stepping away to try and be happy,
I only doomed myself further.

First Meeting

Like an imaginary backstage pass
in the philosophy of survival,
do you remember the day?
when you first met
both of my girls, Sarah
for the first time?,

setting off both
of our emotional alarms that morning
proclaiming you weren't sure
what if they both hated me?
and would tell their mother
my now ex wife to take them away?

I didn't know, of course
so instead lied completely
hoping for the best
'You love me, don't you?
they are both like me
just female and younger'

Neither were like me, of course
Melissa was the spit of her mother
right down to her tempter
while Nicola was more like my father
her hands always buried in science books
and the back garden.

Of course, they both loved you
and likely were worrying the same
in a ripple of ill wind at the fair
all that afternoon
trending your jeans underfoot
trying to keep up with them

making fun of everything
having the time of your lives
in opposite corners of the room.

Homesick

Travelling in opposite directions
do you remember, Sarah?
the chaos of those first few months
when my unpublished novel
nearly became a film
and I was in Coventry one day
then Edinburgh the next,

strolling past cities
on a daily basis on the train
leaving you wondering
what you had stepped into
when I should have been
just a few days away
became a week then a month

living two separate lives
hundreds of miles apart
one buried in sales
the other in tourism
those phone calls every night
which could easily split have split us
 neither of us knew.

Do you remember that day? Sarah
when I eventually returned;
everything withdrawn
and I was back where I started
changing the rhythm of my career
in the space of a little over
just a few months,

our lives lost in-between,
almost from the beginning
sculpted in parallel evolutions
stashed in separate lives
braced against different emotions
barely edging above the waves
until a slot can be found together.

Between yesterday and today, or somewhere further afield

Do you remember what lies beyond that garden?
and the hill across the side road, Sarah
or whether the sea breeze in the distance
leads another way to the black cliff,

Do you remember if the hill led back to town?
or towards that broken country path
laced in daffodils in the cracks
stopping at the edge of the meadows.

Was it Spring or Summer
or a hazy memory somewhere between
and did horses run free across there?
like a tractor in a mechanical indifference

shifting metres in moments
between yesterday and before we met again
streaked through the estuary
corroded in the waves

crawling across memories
ebbing into reflection for a few seconds
immersing ourselves in childhood again
and dawn turned into daylight.

Between then and there, everything disintegrated.

Between then and now
would the meaning of that painting changed
instead of just padlocking yourself in grief
without realising it was just an attempt
to cheer you up after your father died.

It wasn't either of our faults
he had been cheating for years
and had died in that other woman's arms
nor was it the painter's fault.
when you told her bluntly to go and stick one,

Do you remember me telling yourself
I liked the yellow at the edge of the plants.
which contrasted nicely with the use of the hands
only for you to then storm off on the pair of us
and have the painters almost burst into tears.

I picture that poor woman even now
stunned at your outburst
and the way you slammed shut the door
leaving us both stunned.
and me feeling like I had to buy it.

Do you remember the rows it caused? Sarah
when I first hung it in our kitchen
before eventually next to our front door
rolling the metre back in time
Every time I open the door,

opening memories, some perhaps best forgotten
every-time I look at that painting years later.
and you were screaming as I held my head in shock
as your mental health slowly started
to completely disintegrate.

Church Closure at Guide Bridge

The slates are gone from the wall
outside the church
where we got married, Sarah
and the padlock on the front door
that kept the world outside
from sneaking a look after it closed.

The asile where you stood there
and said you would love me forever
a cat has clearly messed on
and one of the windows
on the roof
has been damaged by a storm.

Your absence inches forward
the blown down headstones
and the two trees over the side door
leading back into the church
when your older sister realised
she had left her coat behind.

You would be shocked, Sarah
over how things have changed since then
and would be shocked
in the state it was being left in
until your memory stares at me
in a ripple of ill wind,

and the fact that everybody
rushed off as quickly as possible
wounding our day
with imaginary stones
like they were counting down
as soon as you said yes.

Your brother's funeral

Do you think,, looking back, Sarah
your brother was being serious
with the Laurel and Hardy theme
being played at his funeral
or was it like
done as a half arsed joke
like the rest of his lifetime
seemed to be.

We both knew
after your father died
he had been depressed
God knows how long;
heaving off
in different directions
either more than normal
every Friday and Saturday night.

Do you remember that last time, Sarah
we saw that Christmas
and he would barely say a word
to either of your sisters or your Mum
let alone us
and just saw looking out the window
as if in a snapshot.

'Is he okay?' I can remember asking you
only for you to shake your head
your face reversed by the light
vaproised in regret for weeks afterwards
we were unable to spot the signs earlier
living us both staring upwards in shock
tearing us apart within months.

Facing Shipley Woods

That moment of sunshine
covering the ticket office
at the start of each morning
over Guide Bridge
always reminds me of you, Sarah
when you used to leave for work
each morning towards the end dejected
clearly not in the mood

and then only a few hours later
when you get home
and I was buried in my agent calls
and you would stand in the kitchen
bucking your emotions
in almost a receptacle of regret
waiting patiently for me to finish
unable to tell me how unhappy you were

giving yourself a breathing space
a resolution to what I was thinking
was just another bad day at work
do you remember me asking, Sarah
only for you to nod your head
in a sigh that I missed completely
floating straight back out of the door
which you followed shortly after.

Your Records

Like your father before you
it wasn't much to show
Was it Sarah?
just a box of clothes
and a mismash of Oremonts
mostly from Blackpool
from the life you lived
before and after
we were married.

Your records were the worst
lined up in a row
your younger sister said
like your father's before that
with Marvin Gaye's Here, My Dear
sitting awkwardly next to
Neilson's without you
examining our relationship
almost from the start to the end.

Like your father before you
it wasn't much to show
was it Sarah?
even with any kind of goodbye
after taking them out of her car
almost like
she was glad to be rid.

Your records were the key to you
as a person I can see now
from Lou Reed's 'Transformer'
and dancing badly I have to say
to 'Perfect Day' then 'Love will tear us apart'
by Joy Divsion
without realising it's meaning
all the way through.
until after we had split.

Your records were an extension
of what you really wanted out of life
and the guilt you felt
about the actions
of both of your father
and how it affected your brother
shackling your guilt
into voyeurs of yourselves
that I never saw until after you had died.

Three visits to Paris ten years apart

The first time do you remember, Sarah
it rained all weekend
all the way from the airport in Paris
right up to the Saint Laurent
on our honeymoon
and we spent most of the afternoon
well into the evening
in the Latin Quarter
listening to a jazz band
which you couldn't stand.

Five years later
and three after contracting diabetes
do you remember, Sarah
having to almost mesmerise me in guilt
to get me on that plane
exhausted after the collapse
of another adaptation of my book
and nearly losing Michelle
during the birth of her first child
three weeks earlier.

Five years after
and two after you had died,
the guilt follows me out
off the airport
on a cheap stopover to Milan
at the edge of the Seine,
a blank interior
to days gone past
as much as words
that could still be said.

Five years after
and two after you had gone
of untold stories stood there
and perpetual sadness
with the rain
lost in the brilliance of memory
an effigy in emoition
disappeared into the past
echoing the silence
of your goodbye to my mouth.

After Leaving

You wanted to be a poet too,
do you remember telling me once Sarah
and I always thought
you would write a book in rage
after our marriage collapsed
instead of a little more than a
a few half-scribbled verses
around the back of your sofa.

You wanted to be a poet too,
do you remember telling me once Sarah
writing book after book of poetry
studying eternity
flung out across the ocean
through a telescope
in contrast to the cinematic nature
I wrote both my novels and scripts.

Your poems instead counted down
from 4, 3, 2 right to 1
in emotional rage
rather than words
without either of us realising
as soon as I got diabetes
and I was unable to be the husband
I think you expected me to be.

Our marriage descending
into a sacrificed silence
with every trip I had to make,
every reading I ended up making
becoming like another shard
from an emotional shrapnel
you would begin to stab yourself
that eventually drove us apart,

Your love becoming a vacuum.
after first your father and then your brother died
and whatever you felt began
to tear itself away within you
as I simply didn't have the energy
and you eventually walked away
your guilt turning into an hourglass,
then a chiming claw,

rather than a rage over poetry.

Going to your funeral in Radcliffe

Before disappearing into the sunlight
did you see me Sarah arriving late
after everybody had arrived
on the afternoon of your funeral
wherever you have ended up,

Curled up in a corner
holding a glass of wine
afterwards in the York
next to Bolton Bus train station
then the Sweet Green Tavern.

Leaving notes mentally
everywhere I went without realising
counting down the days to this
until we got to that last night
and we split for the last time

You always gave me the
performance of lifetime
do you remember me saying
before heading back into the shadows
it was a shame I couldn't keep up

First in Brighton
Southport, York,
London, Birmingham
our performances were never on stage
but across back street pubs

And even after we got married
stitching our interests together
into mis-shaped tablecloths
built up from garbled lust
it was never enough

Flaking up clues from
the bitterness from your family
who wouldn't look me in the eye
after I arrived at your funeral late
barely able to look at anybody

You always knew it would end this way
didn't you, Sarah that moment
you walked back into my life
in Bar Italia in Brighton
all those years before?

You knew, didn't you, Sarah
even if you couldn't tell me at the time
building up Curtain Call after Curtain Call
over each town or city we visited
and every adventure I was a party to

Was it Bolton when I became Diabetic
when things changed between the pair of us
and I was unable to do what I used to do
forcing us to step into a new scene
and it changed both of us

Or Blackpool, when I was left wondering
for at least five days after we got home
what had you done to get us to that room
and what you said
to me in Fleetwood afterwards.

I should have known in Shipley Woods
and I saw the guilt in your face
that last night when in the snow
and you would barely
talk to me all the way home

And that morning in Radcliffe
before taxing over to Bolton
like it was the last place on Earth
raining down on my regrets
into an acid black dusk.

Cast out into an emotional climax of silence
when I got back on the train back home
Watercolour in differing sunsets
screensavers tied to
my thoughts in regrets.

Dabbing rain clouds over the sun
getting off the train home
and walking through the front door
like a closed concert hall
stitched together in words

Forever changing carriages in Birmingham
across a mouthful of sorries
Knowing given the choice
I would do it all again.

Biography:

Andy N is the author of ten poetry collections, the last being 'Changing Carriages at Birmingham New Street' and co-runs Chorlton Cum Hardy's always welcoming spoken word open mic night 'Speak Easy'.

He run/co-runs the Podcasts 'Spoken Label' and 'Cloaked in the Shadows' and does ambient music under names such as Ocean in a Bottle, Polly Ocean and Mandy in a Bottle.

His website is:
https://onewriterandhispc.blogspot.com/

His substack page is:
https://andyn.substack.com/

* Coming soon *

Step into the mesmerizing world of "Birth," the debut novel by Manchester-based poet, podcaster, and ambient musician, Andy N.

Delve deep into the psyche of a young writer as this extraordinary tale offers a poetic, sad, and often hilarious portrait of his coming-of-age journey as his creativity is almost literally dragged out of him into the beginning of his journey as a poet, into fronting a five-piece acoustic band, and so much more.

In this captivating narrative, the reader is taken on a profound exploration of the writer's upbringing, skillfully woven with evocative prose that casts a spellbinding charm. "Birth" is a novel where the young writer's world is painted with a palette of feelings, where joy and sorrow dance hand in hand, and humor is found even in the darkest corners.

"Birth" is more than just a novel; it is an ode to the human spirit, a celebration of the written word, and a testament to the resilience of the creative soul.

So, open the cover and step into the world of "Birth," where the boundaries between reality and fiction fade, and the heart of a young writer beats with unyielding passion. What happens next is a testament to the magic of storytelling and the boundless potential of a pen.

Also available:

In the Midst of Winter
Andy N

Embracing different challenges, In the Midst of Winter, the new book by Andy N is his third seasonal book following from 'The End of Summer' and 'The Birth of Autumn' is as much the story of what comes next heading into Winter as much as a gathering of thoughts of what led there whether in the middle of a snow storm or looking at frost on windowpanes.

In the Midst of Winter is a study of silence whether with nature or in the winter of your memories and a in-depth of our relationships with everywhere in the middle.

In the Midst of Winter is a poetry book looking for light in the darkness, the light switch across the storms and the snow that dominates our excitmenet and worry often in the same breath.

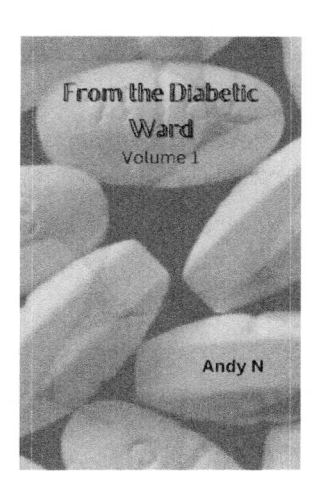

From the Diabetic Ward, the new poetry collection by Andy N is his more personal book yet detailing the events when he first contracted Diabetes back in 2011.

This collection is a frank examination of how things changed overnight when his feet whipped out from underneath him changing everything from his writing, relationship, work, and everything in between overnight.

From the Diabetic Ward is a poetry book that looks at cracks within emotions and how becoming Diabetic forces you to re-evaluate life from everything from the way you sleep, eat, work, and operate in a relationship and as a writer how you write and breathe your words.

This collection is an awakening call, a study of before and after and how a major change in your life does not mean the end but rather a new beginning at the point when it appears that everything is over.

Dock Leaves the latest poetry collection by Andy N, the author of 'Return to Kemptown' and 'The End of Summer' among others is his most personal collection of poetry to date.

Wrote over a ten year period between 2012 to 2022 when working in the back office of a United Kingdom court building now closed, Dock Leaves is a study of stories that looks at the very essence of Justice through all sides of the story from the people on trial, the families caught in-between and the court staff who have to deliver justice after sentence has being announced.

Dock Leaves is a insight to the minds of all involved from a completely different point of view talking about justice that goes beyond a simple black or white or guilty or not guilty – instead going in-between the lines like a newspaper reporter looking for answers in ways that haven't being reported before.

Dock Leaves is more than a insight of justice, rather stories within stories that happen in the most extreme told with humour and pathos and stories within stories, emotions within emotions and instead of counting 4, 3, 2 to 1.

The Frog With No Friends

Amanda Nicholson

A lonely frog named Hoppy finds an unlikely friendship with a kind-hearted snake named Slither. Together, they learn that appearances don't matter, and friendship can be found in unexpected places.

Join Hoppy and Slither as they explore the wonders of nature, chase fireflies, and build cherished memories that will last a lifetime. With delightful illustrations and a message of acceptance, this charming children's book celebrates the power of friendship and the joy of embracing our differences.

Printed in Great Britain
by Amazon